The Pocket Weather Forecaster
by Dr. Simon Keeling PhD, MSc, FRMETs

CONTENTS

Introduction & Acknowledgements

The weather has a huge impact on outdoor activities; sailing, flying, farming, fishing, walking, golfing, or even a trip to the seaside are all affected by atmospheric behaviour. Many of us observe changes in cloud formations, but few understand the significance. Clouds are like crystal balls in the air, they foretell the weather of the coming hours and, when their significance is recognised, can give fair warning of impending conditions.

You don't require a degree in meteorology to understand weather, simply the ability to look and feel what the weather is doing around you at any one time. It is our understanding of changes in these "feelings" which can help to predict the weather.

I have therefore written this book to be a handy pick-up guide to the main formations of cloud. It should be useful in identifying cloud types and therefore in helping one assess what weather they may foretell.

As a self-confessed weather anorak, I would like to thank all of those who attend my regular Weather School training days for suggesting ideas for this book, as well as those who received my regular Weekend Forecast and Weather Musings, delivered by email (see http://www.weatherweb.net). Also, thanks must be extended to Ian Collins (Weatherpictures.co.uk) for allowing me to use so many of his wonderful pictures (pages 17, 27, 45, 47 and 65).

Above all though, I must thank Kathryn, Elizabeth and Daisy for putting up with my obsessive ramblings about the weather for so many years.

Simon Keeling

How do you feel today?

The human body is the best weather forecaster, so every time you walk out of the door ask yourself, "how does it feel today?". Is the air feeling cold or hot? Is there a breeze blowing? Is the air dry or moist? By answering these questions, and applying some very simple rules of physics one can gather plenty of information about what the air around us is doing.

Remember the following rules of thumb:

- Warm air can hold more moisture than cold air.
- Colder air holds less moisture.
- The faster the temperature decreases with height (lapse rate) the more unstable the air.

- Air flows from high to low pressure.
- Winds blow anti-clockwise around low pressure, clockwise around high pressure.
- What goes up must come down.

- Cold air is dense, warm air is less dense.

By "feeling" the weather and using the above rules one can produce a simple, yet effective forecast, especially when adding the information that clouds can give.

Beaufort Scale

The Beaufort scale enables easy estimation of wind speed and can be used on land, or at sea.

Force	Description	Speed knots	Speed mph	On Land	At Sea
0	Calm	<1	<1	Calm; smoke rises vertically.	Sea like a mirror.
1	Light air	1-3	1-3	Wind vanes don't move.	Ripples, no foam crests.
2	Light breeze	4-6	4-7	Wind felt on face, leaves rustle.	Small wavelets, crests don't break.
3	Gentle breeze	7-10	8-12	Leaves & small twigs in motion.	Large wavelets, crests begin to break.
4	Moderate breeze	11-16	13-18	Raises dust & loose paper.	Fairly frequent white horses.
5	Fresh breeze	17-21	19-24	Small trees in leaf begin to sway.	Moderate waves, many white horses.
6	Strong breeze	22-27	25-31	Large branches in motion.	Large waves, extensive foam crests.
7	Near gale	28-33	32-38	Whole trees in motion.	White foam blown in streaks.
8	Gale	34-40	39-46	Breaks twigs of trees.	Moderately high waves.
9	Strong gale	41-47	47-54	Chimney pots & slates blown off.	High waves, dense foam streaks.
10	Storm	48-55	55-63	Trees uprooted, structural damage.	Very high waves. Sea looks "white".
11	Violent storm	56-63	64-72	Rare, widespread damage.	Exceptionally high waves.
12	Hurricane	>64	>73	-	Air filled with foam and spray.

The winds doth blow (but where's the low)?

The wind is simply air moving from one place to another. On the previous page I mentioned air flowing from regions of high to low pressure. Exactly the same principle applies when you use a vacuum cleaner. The cleaner lowers pressure inside the machine, creating a partial vacuum. This results in air outside the machine (which is under higher pressure) flowing into the vacuum cleaner, thus making all of our lives cleaner! (although I recall the time, much to my shame, when my wife was away and I had to ask our neighbour where the on/off switch was for the vacuum cleaner!).

Wind can tell us where high and low pressure systems are relative to our current position on the Earth's surface. This is called Buys Ballot's Law and it states:

▲ Stand with your back to the wind (in the Northern Hemisphere) and low pressure will always be on your left hand side.

The law works every time, and I must admit that when single point forecasting it is a very useful little trick to know. Until a few years back ships at sea relied only on the data available via HF radio. These signals could vary and so on-board meteorologists had to count on their own intuition and laws such as these in order to make predictions.

It's in front of you!

A front marks the boundary between two air masses (see page 10). The front is simply an aide to understand the weather chart, but given some guidance, it is possible to deduce the weather that is likely to be caused as a front passes overhead. There are three main types of front; warm, cold and occluded.

Warm front

Depicted on charts by a red line with a semi-circle, the warm front generally precedes a cold front. Typical cloud sequences ahead of the warm front are Cirrus-Cirrostratus-Altocumulus-Altostratus-Nimbostratus. As the front passes the cloud becomes Stratus.

Rain will usually start falling when cloud reaches the Altostratus stage, turning heavier at Nimbostratus and then more drizzly in Stratus, perhaps lasting 4 hours. Winds generally back ahead of the front, then veer as it passes. A rise in temperature is noticed as the front passes.

Cold front

Following the warm front is usually a cold front, depicted on charts as a blue triangle. Typical cloud sequences ahead of the front are Stratus (from the remnants of the warm front) then Cumulonimbus/Cumulus. As the front passes there may be a brief spell of heavy rain and the possibility of a crack of thunder. Once the front has moved through skies may become clear for an hour or two, before cumulus return possibly bringing some heavy showers. Rain will usually be heavy, although lasting only an hour or two.

Occluded front

Where a cold and warm front meets an occluded front is formed, shown as a purple line with semicircles and triangles. The cloud and weather sequence associated with the occlusion is similar to a cold front.

Remember that on all charts the triangles and semicircles point in the direction that the front is moving.

Pressure systems

The charts seen on television, the internet or in our daily newspaper can be very useful when forecasting. They show low pressure and high pressure, as well as fronts. By identifying the typical weather brought by these systems, one can gain a greater understanding as to the weather over the coming hours. Here are some symbols you may see on charts.

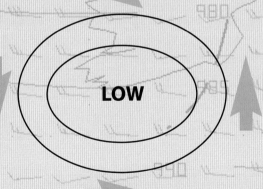

Winds flow in an anti-clockwise directions around low pressure. Poor weather is associated with low pressure including rain, drizzle and strong winds.

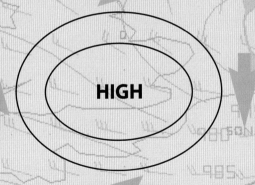

Winds flow clockwise around high pressure areas. Summer highs bring fine conditions and sunshine, whilst winter highs can cause overnight frosts and daytime cloud.

Formation of clouds

Whether you're looking at a huge storm cloud, or grey, featureless skies on a dull day in winter, clouds are made up of the same thing: condensed water vapour (or ice). They vary in size and shape from a few metres to many hundreds of miles across.

Clouds form when air rises and cools. Water vapour within the parcel of rising air condenses on minute particles in the atmosphere. These particles can be pollution, dust or even sea salt. We see the condensed water vapour in the form of clouds. There are two types of cloud; **convective** and **stratiform**.

Convective clouds (may cause showers)

These are some of the most familiar cloud types. They range from the small, fluffy cumulus cloud, to the gigantic cumulonimbus thunderstorm cloud. Their formation is triggered by the atmosphere being heated. Air can then rise, often imagined in the form of a bubble. Provided that the air the bubble rises into is colder than the bubble, the bubble will continue to rise. When the bubble can no longer hold the water vapour within it as a vapour, condensation takes place and a cloud is born. The cloud will then continue to rise, perhaps developing rain and hail until it encounters warmer surrounding air. A "flat top" may then be seen, known as an 'anvil'.

Stratiform clouds (may bring rain)

These clouds bring us more persistent rain, drizzle, or perhaps even just a rather dull day. The clouds are formed when air is forced to rise. This may be because of air encountering a mountain range, or perhaps even another front. Should the clouds rise far enough, or contain enough water vapour, they may produce rain or drizzle.

Classification of cloud

You will already know that clouds occur at different heights in the atmosphere. All clouds that bring weather of significance occur within the layer of air know as the troposphere, which extends to about 12km. Jet aircraft fly above this layer to avoid the worst of any weather.

There are occasions when clouds can extend beyond the troposphere and into the next layer, the stratosphere. These clouds are called cumulonimbus clouds and more is explained about these later. But there is another type of cloud which occurs very high in the atmosphere. These clouds are called noctilucent clouds and can only be seen when illuminated by sunlight from below.

Of course, the clouds we are interested in are much lower down. By international convention they are broken down into three height regimes:

Low Clouds - Surface to 6500ft

Medium Clouds - 6500ft to 23,000ft

High Clouds - 16,500ft to 45,000ft

When defining the height of clouds we are referring to the height of their base. It may be that the tops of the cloud extend much higher into the atmosphere than this, for example a large cumulonimbus cloud may reach in excess of 50,000ft.

Where has the warm air come from?

Air masses

If you can identify the origin of the air that is overhead at any one time, and estimate how this air might have been changed as it was blown towards the current location, one can make a pretty good guess as to what weather such air might bring. Conveniently we can classify types of air depending upon where they originated and the weather they bring: we call these types of air 'air masses'.

Tropical Maritime

This is air that arrives in the British Isles on a south-westerly wind. The air has originated in the tropical regions, suggesting that it is warm. The air travels over the Atlantic (hence the maritime suffix), picking up moisture as it goes. By the time it reaches our shores it is frequently completely saturated and brings low cloud, mist, fog and rain to western coasts. Inland areas usually have plenty of cloud, but this can break allowing some warm sunshine to come through, especially in the summer months over more eastern and central areas of England and Scotland.

Stratus and nimbostratus cloud are most frequently associated with the Tropical Maritime air mass.

Tropical Continental

When air travels from the south to the British Isles it passes over the dry landmass of Europe. As the air moves north it becomes increasingly dry and warm. As it reaches the British Isles it brings plenty of clear skies. This leads to lots of sunshine through many areas and some very warm and even hot temperatures through the summer months.

Cirrus is the cloud most frequently associated with Tropical Continental air.

Where has the cold air come from?

Polar Maritime
You might guess from its name that this air mass starts life in the Polar regions. It travels southwards towards the British Isles, crossing the north-east Atlantic, north-west of Scotland. Clouds are generated and by the time the air mass reaches the country it contains showers. Polar Maritime air gives some beautifully clear skies between showers. It can produce snow showers during the winter months with northern and western areas most likely to see these. Very few make it to the southeast of the country,

Arctic Maritime
With the word 'maritime' in its name you will not be surprised to learn that this air mass passes over the sea. This time the air originates in the Arctic Ocean, north of Scandinavia. It travels to the British Isles from the northeast. Having a fairly long sea track over an often frozen sea, the air mass does not warm up on its journey south. It brings wintry showers to eastern parts of the country during the winter months, some of them heavy. More western areas are drier although everywhere will be bitterly cold during winter.

Polar Continental
Originating at the Pole, but this time passing over the land mass of Scandinavia and Russia, this air mass arrives in the British Isles from the east. It brings dry weather (apart from some low cloud, fog and showers on eastern coasts), whilst western areas are brighter with sunshine.

Returning Polar Maritime
Brought about by slow moving low pressure west of Ireland, cold Polar Maritime is forced south over the warmer Atlantic. Here it generates heavier showers and then returns them back to the British Isles from the southwest as frequent, heavy and sometimes persistent showers.

High Clouds

Cirrus
Cirrostratus
Cirrocumulus

13

Cirrus

"Tuft or Curl of Hair"

15

Cirrus
Indicating No Change

These cirrus clouds are typical of a summers day. Forming high in the atmosphere (above 18,000 feet) the clouds are described in official meteorological texts as being like filaments or twisted hooks.

Watch cirrus clouds carefully as they can indicate an approaching warm front, or if viewed on the horizon could be associated with a cumulonimbus cloud.

Should these clouds not increase, or turn into cirrostratus they are likely to indicate very little change in the weather for at least the next six hours.

Cirrus
Indicating an Improvement

Cirrus may follow the passage of a cold front and therefore indicate an improvement in conditions.

This picture was taken following the clearance of a cold front and clearly shows the cumulonimbus and cumulus cloud that was associated with the fronts passage through the photograph region.

A typical cold front passage brings a rise in pressure and a period of more settled weather. Another tell-tale sign of the passage of a cold front is a dramatic improvement in visibility. This fine weather usually lasts between one and three hours, after this time showers are likely as cumulus clouds develop as cold air advances aloft. Some of the showers could be heavy and thundery.

Cirrus
Indicating a Deterioration

When watching cirrus the question uppermost in your mind should be "Is this cloud associated with a warm front?".

Very often the cirrus will begin to thicken into cirrostratus. That is what is happening in the picture opposite. The spectacular cirrus formation in the centre of the picture draws the eye, but take a look out to sea. Notice that the cloud is becoming more 'flattened' and thicker. This is an area of encroaching cirrostratus cloud. In this situation one should watch the cirrus clouds closely for signs of further thickening to cirrostratus.

If the thickening of the cloud continues rain may follow this stage within 4 to 8 hours, depending on the speed of movement of the warm front. In this example rain arrived about five hours after the picture was taken.

Cirrostratus

"Curled and spread out"

23

Cirrostratus
Indicating No Change

It is rare that cirrostratus cloud would appear independent of other cloud types, and indicate no change in coming conditions.

Only when cirrostratus are part of a very slow moving frontal system could the observer believe that no change in conditions during the next six hours was likely. Generally, cirrostratus cloud is part of an established weather system and therefore would normal indicate that a change is on the way. It generally follows cirrus, thickening into altostratus.

Cirrostratus clouds can produce a halo around the moon or sun, these can be spectacular, although may only be short lived.

Cirrostratus
Indicating an Improvement

Cirrostratus cloud may well follow the passage of a front. Previous to this picture being taken rain had been falling for several hours. However, the rain cleared before dawn skies cleared somewhat and mist and fog patches formed.

The front was not a well defined feature and so had a significant hang-back of cloud, of which the cirrostratus was part. One should watch for this cloud clearing because if it is following a cold front the clearance of the cloud may indicate that the atmosphere is becoming more unstable and that showers may form in the coming hours.

A sign of any shower development would be the appearance of small cumulus clouds (see page 66).

Cirrostratus
Indicating a Deterioration

Sometimes, if cirrostratus is present, a halo may form around the sun or moon.

As the cirrostratus thickens the halo may become more noticeable, perhaps with mock suns appearing to the sides of the sun or moon (as the one to the far left of the photograph shown on the opposite page).

Approximately four hours after this photograph was taken, cloud had thickened sufficiently and rain began to fall.

Cirrocumulus

"Curled mass"

Cirrocumulus

Cirrocumulus cloud is one of the most illusive of all the clouds.

The cloud does not really give many indications as to what the weather will do over the coming hours, although it should be watched for any developments into altocumulus, which could indicate more widespread instability in the atmosphere.

It is often seen after the passage of a warm front, especially during the summer months.

By it's nature cirrocumulus can indicate instability at high levels in the atmosphere.

Medium Clouds

Altocumulus
Altostratus

Altocumulus

"High masses"

Altocumulus
Indicating No Change

Residing in the medium levels of the atmosphere, usually between 6500ft and 18,000ft, altocumulus clouds make for some striking sunrise and sunsets.

If the cloud is well 'dappled' and ragged in appearance with little other cloud around, it frequently means that the weather is likely to stay stable for the coming hours.

The picture opposite was taken early on a January morning. The altocumulus cloud followed a clear night, and was a patch of cloud which traversed the location within approximately twenty minutes. The remainder of the morning was dry and bright with sunny spells.

During the summer months one should watch the clouds for signs of any vertical development as this could indicate the onset of showers or thunderstorms.

Altocumulus Indicating
Showers & Thunderstorms

Altocumulus is indicative of an unstable atmosphere. Watch the altocumulus clouds for any signs of vertical development.

Sometimes this vertical development can become pronounced, the altocumulus clouds then becoming altocumulus castellanus, literally mean 'castle'. And that's exactly how these clouds appear, as the turrets of a castle.

If the altocumulus castellanus clouds continue to grow then this is a sure sign that showers or thunderstorms are on the way.

Altocumulus Associated with a Warm Front

As a warm front approaches the cirrus cloud thickens to cirrostratus, and eventually altocumulus.

The altocumulus cloud that is part of the warm frontal system does not usually produce any precipitation; this is reserved for the altostratus which you can see encroaching below the altocumulus on the picture opposite.

One should be aware that altocumulus can develop into castellanus cloud which, if they become thick enough, can produce rain and can also foretell of developing thunderstorms or heavy showers (see page 40).

43

Altostratus

"A high blanket"

Altostratus
Indicating No Change

Sometimes moisture can become 'trapped' in the middle levels of the atmosphere giving the appearance of a fairly grey day.

These areas of altostratus are definitely at a lower level than cirrus or cirrostratus clouds, but are usually at a sufficient altitude to make them discernable as a medium level cloud.

There is no real way to be absolutely sure that altostratus is innocuous, apart from actually watching the cloud over time. If it develops following cirrus, cirrostratus and altocumulus then it is a good indication that the cloud is associated with a warm front but, if like the cloud opposite, it is part of a layer which has not changed or developed over time, it can be taken that the weather will not change much during the next few hours. Note that some fog is also shown in the picture, this later lifted to stratus cloud (see page 54).

Altostratus
Indicating Gusty Winds

Sometimes a warm front can lose much of its lower level cloud. This may be because the winds blow against high ground, such as when strong southwest winds blow into the Welsh mountains. The rainfall associated with the cloud is deposited on the windward side of the hills, the air is then forced to rise and is dried out further, warming as it descends the other side of the mountains.

This action can sometimes lead to a cap of cloud being displayed in medium levels of the atmosphere. Such a cloud is know as Lenticularis (no surprise when you see the lens shape of the cloud).

If this cloud is visible it can predict strong and gusty winds on the leeward side of the hills. Pilots, sailors and walkers should be aware that winds may gust significantly above those experienced in the area away from the hills or mountains.

Altostratus
Indicating a Deterioration

As the cloud which follows altocumulus as a warm front approaches, altostratus cloud is more usually associated with rain.

It is altostratus which can produce one of the most beautiful effects of the warm front; the halo. As we have already seen, cirrostratus cloud can also produce a halo effect, but the altostratus halo is often more definite.

The cloud will be thickening all the time, and eventually the sun or moon will become a faint spot of light, a little like looking at a light through ground glass. The direction from which the halo breaks is the direction from which rain is approaching.

Producing the first rain of the warm front altostratus heralds a period of rain lasting several hours. Winds will also increase and the air pressure will fall.

Low Clouds

Stratus
Nimbostratus
Stratocumulus
Cumulus
Cumulonimbus

Stratus

"Stretched and spread-out"

Stratus

Stratus cloud is low, featureless cloud. It can occur anywhere from the surface of the ground (when it is known as fog) up to about 1200ft into the air.

It is usually a thin type of cloud and can only produce drizzle. If it is raining, and you have stratus cloud overhead, this is because another cloud is above the stratus cloud causing the rain. This effect is known as 'seeding'.

Stratus cloud can occur widely behind a warm front and is the low cloud that brings so much damp weather in a Tropical Maritime air mass.

On mornings when fog has occurred one should watch for the winds increasing slightly, lifting the fog from the surface. This can form a layer of low stratus cloud which may take a time to burn away, and in some circumstances during the winter months may last all day.

Stratocumulus

"A spread-out mass"

Stratocumulus

Stratocumulus indicates that the atmosphere is in a stable state. This means that there is not much happening weatherwise and that the temperature of the atmosphere does not fall a great deal, or perhaps even rises, with height.

The height of stratocumulus cloud is normally between about 1500ft and 6500ft. As the cloud is not very thick it can only really produce light rain or drizzle. If it is raining heavily then this means that there must be other, thicker cloud above it.

Breaks frequently occur in stratocumulus cloud allowing the sun or moon to shine through. If you have stratocumulus cloud overhead then there is unlikely to be significant change in the weather for the next couple of hours.

Nimbostratus

"Rain blanket"

Nimbostratus

'Nimbo' means 'rain' and that is exactly what nimbostratus cloud brings. It is nimbostratus which produces the rainfall associated with warm fronts. This dark, grey blanket shrouds hill sides. The base of the cloud is ragged with   fingers of moisture hanging well below the main cloud base.

Occurring anywhere from the surface to 6500ft nimbostratus can extend high into the atmosphere, in excess of 15,000ft in the most active frontal systems. Generally the cloud will occur close to a warm front, ahead of the actually passage of the front. Once the front has passed through the cloud usually thins to stratus and the rain becomes lighter and drizzly.

Walkers and pilots should be aware that nimbostratus cloud can quickly cover the hills and coasts, frequently hiding the tops of mountain ranges.

Cumulus

"Heaped clouds"

Cumulus
Indicating No Change

All cumulus type clouds are formed by convection. If the morning is a fine and sunny one and small cumulus clouds start to develop, watch for a few minutes and see if they begin to extend upwards. Similarly, if it is a fine day and cumulus clouds appear in the afternoon, watch carefully as they could indicate the start of showers.

Should there be no change in the vertical development of the cumulus clouds, and the tops become rather indistinguishable, such as those shown on the page opposite, this is a good indication that the day should stay fair.

Watch for high cirrus clouds appearing above the cumulus clouds as these may indicate the approach of a warm front.

Cumulus
Indicating an Improvement

There are two ways in which an improvement in the weather can be foretold by cumulus clouds. The first is after a day of showers: on such occasions large cumulus clouds can begin to collapse and almost melt away at sunset (such as the clouds on the opposite page). Here, only the remnants of large cumulus clouds remain. During the preceding hour showers had faded away and the tops of the cloud had become much lower, showing that the showers were finished for the day. The following night would be dry.

The second improvement shown by cumulus clouds is more temporary. If cirrus clouds begin to invade the sky above the cumulus clouds this can often mean that a warm front is on the way. The advancing cirrus clouds bring warm air at high levels and this limits the vertical growth of the cumulus clouds. Any showers will fade away as the clouds reduce in size. The weather may then become fair for a few hours before altostratus cloud arrives bringing the rain associated with the warm front.

Cumulus
Indicating a Deterioration

Watching cumulus for a while can reveal a lot about the potential for the cloud to grow and produce showers. If cumulus clouds are starting to appear in a clear, blue sky then just watch them for a short time. Are they continuing to grow? If so, do they have 'plumes' within them? Are the bases starting to darken? Is cirrus overhead? If so this may mean that the vertical development of the cloud may be interrupted by warmer air aloft and hence the risk of showers could be reduced.

The picture opposite shows a well developed cumulus cloud which is on the verge of becoming cumulonimbus. Notice the plumes with the cloud. This shows that there is significant upward motion taking place. The darkening base is evident too, hinting that heavy showers are imminent.

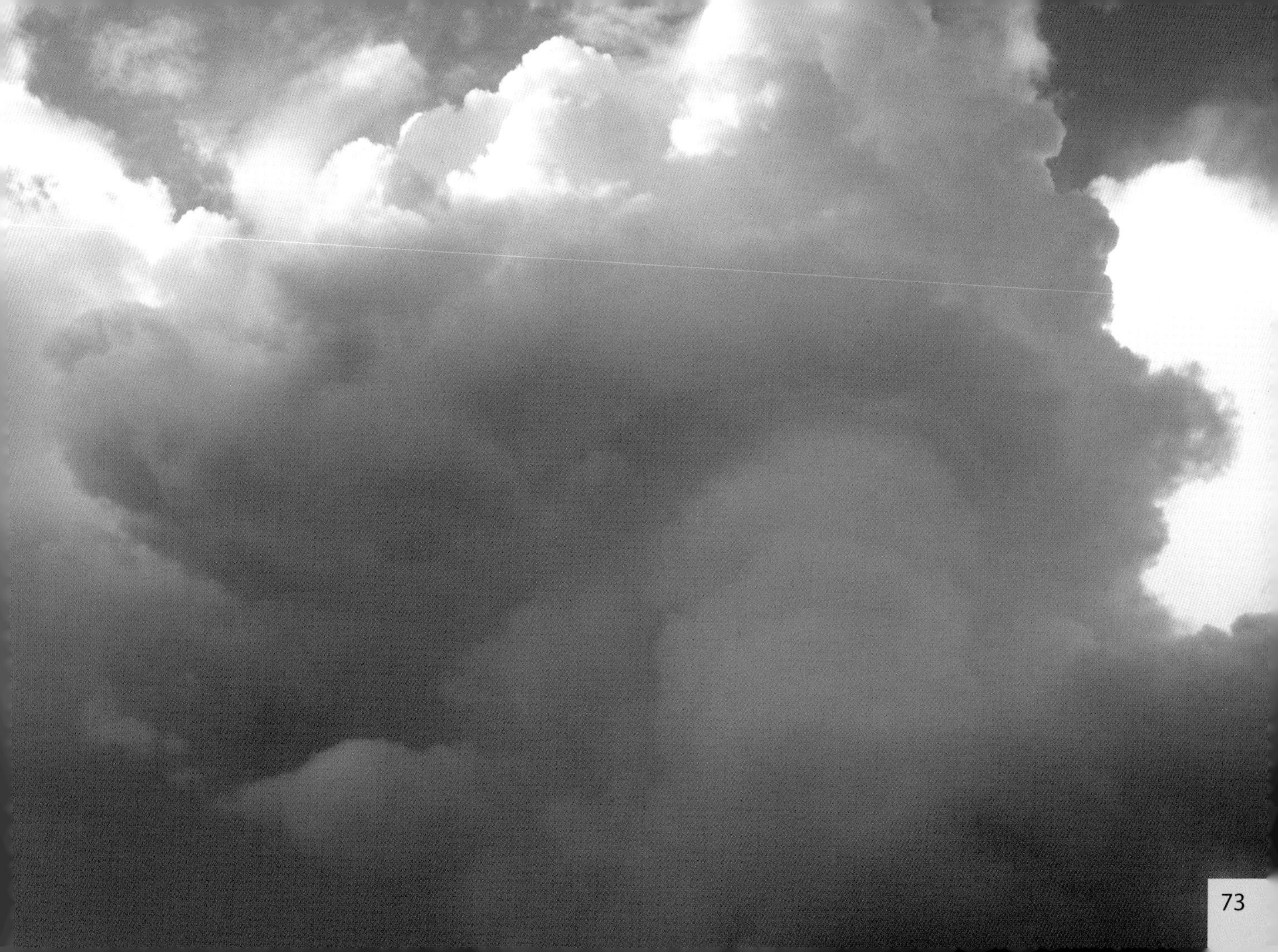

Cumulonimbus

"Mass of rain"

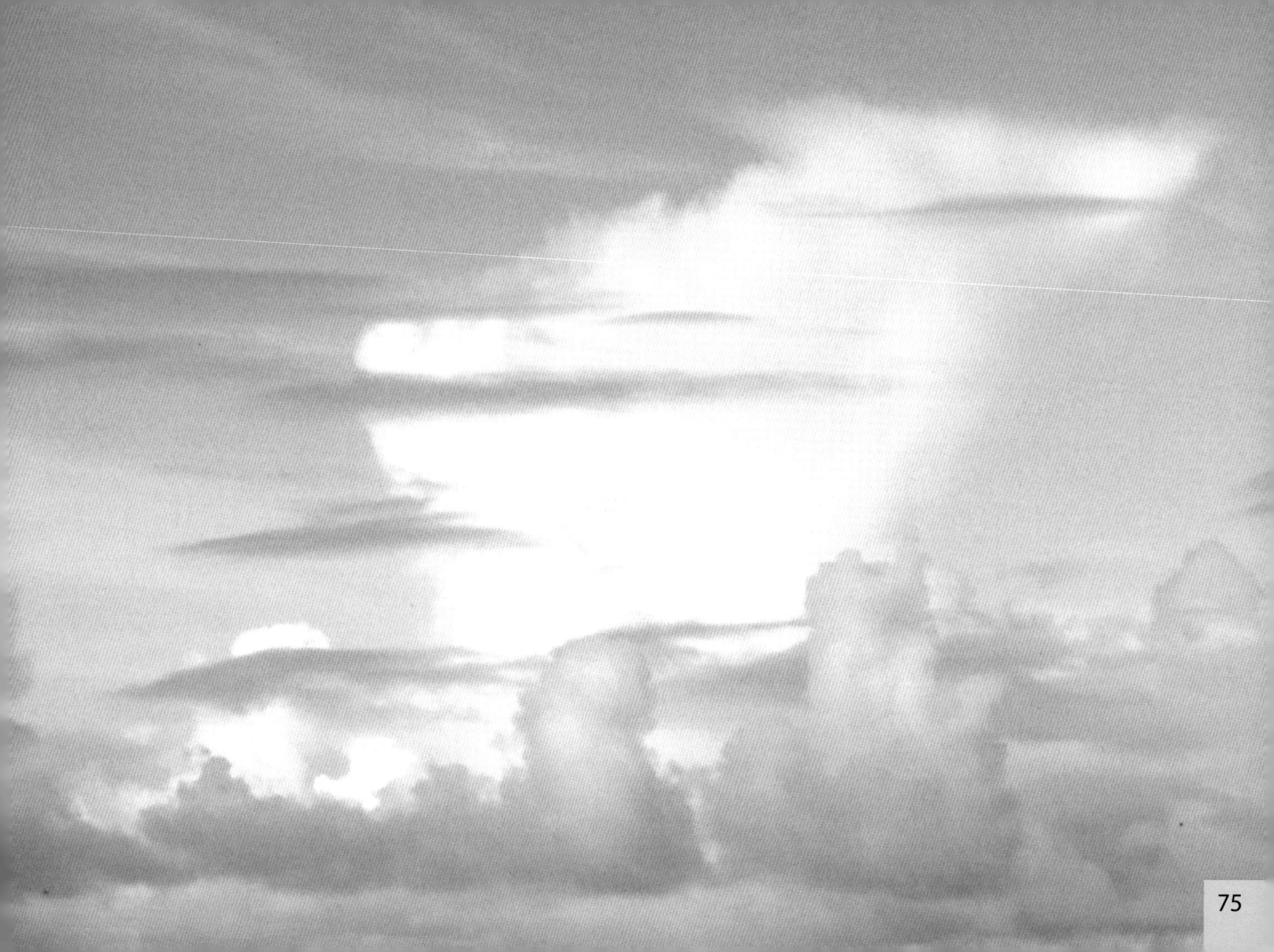

Cumulonimbus
Indicating Heavy Showers

The anvil shaped tops of large cumulonimbus clouds are a sure sign that they are producing showers, and they may be heavy.

This picture shows how the cumulonimbus clouds are often grouped together. Four distinct cumulus towers are clearly visible in the picture, each one of these probably having a heavy shower below it and clearly showing a sequence of showers, then sunshine, then more showers.

In fact, a shower can be seen falling from the shower on the far left of the picture. These cumulonimbus clouds are sufficiently well developed to form thunderstorms and perhaps produce hail (see page 78).

Cumulonimbus
Indicating Thunderstorms

Each of the towers rising through a cumulonimbus clouds is an area of energy ascending through the atmosphere. They show that the cloud is active and it still growing.

In the picture opposite you can see one particular 'puff' of energy rising out of the top of the cloud. Therefore, the cloud is still growing, even though it is raining heavily from the base of the cloud. Note that the cloud has not yet formed an anvil shape at the top and so it clearly has further to climb in the atmosphere as the energy to do so is still available to it.

An observer watching this cloud should start to be aware that despite the loss of energy from the cloud because of rain falling from it, there is still enough energy to make it grow. Therefore there is a good chance that this cloud could produce a thunderstorm.

Cumulonimbus Indicating Squalls, Hail & Tornadoes

Cumulonimbus clouds produce the most violent weather. When the base of the cloud is ragged, such as shown opposite one can ascertain that heavy rain is, or is about to fall from the cloud. Here, heavy rain is falling in the distance, and there is likely to be hail too.

As the cloud approaches the winds will become very gusty, perhaps having been light preceding the clouds arrival. Squally winds can blow in excess of 50mph and are cause by cold air sinking out of the cloud, known as a downdraught or microburst.

Funnel clouds and tornadoes can also form. In conditions such as these watch the base of the cloud for any sign of rotation. The bottom left-hand corner of this picture shows a funnel cloud forming briefly below the main cumulonimbus cloud base.

Conclusion

"It is from books that wise people derive consolation in the troubles of life."

Victor Hugo

The winds doth blow (but where's the low)?

I hope that this book has given you a taste of how the weather works and the information about forthcoming conditions that cloud formations convey.

By watching the skies carefully, identifying clouds, and learning about the weather that follows, you will soon be able to confidently forecast the weather yourself. You could also emulate some of my more enthusiastic correspondents; taking photographs of the clouds and then writing next to them the weather that each type of cloud brought.

Of course, you may also feel that you would like to advance a little further and may start to take measurements using instruments. If this is an avenue that you persue may I recommend that you invest in a good thermometer (there are some excellent digital thermometers available). These will record maximum and minimum temperature, and some give readings of relative humidity too.

Where you chose to site your thermometer is critical. It should be mounted somewhere that is north facing , out of direct sunlight and with the air free to flow around it. If you must attached it to a wall, the wall should be white but do bear in mind that your readings may be compromised by residual heat radiating from the wall.

Take readings at the same time everyday, and before long you will build up a picture of the weather in your locality. Who knows, you may even qualify for a 'weather anorak', just like mine!

Finding out more about the weather with Simon Keeling

Books
Simon Keeling has also written The Sailor's Book of the Weather, published by Wiley. The book is helpful for sailors, and non-sailors alike, who want to delve deeper into the world of Weather. It explains how the weather works and looks at some of the techniques used for making weather forecasts. The book can be purchased at http://www.weatherweb.net

DVD'S
Weather Why's? is a DVD containing many short videos explaining how the weather works. Written by Simon Keeling each video lasts approximately 2 to 5 minutes. Topics covered include air masses, the forming of high and low pressure and the weather they bring, warm fronts and cold fronts, as well as a very useful set of Q & A videos such as 'Why does it rain'. You can purchase the DVD online now at http://www.weatherweb.net

Weather School
"Weather forecasting is a dark art and I want to shine some light on it"; that's how Simon sees Weather School . Run for sailors, climbers, aviators, farmers, TV presenters and just about anyone with an interest in the weather, Weather School provides professional training sessions to help you improve your weather knowledge. Courses run throughout the year, and for more information and the latest course dates please see http://www.weatherschool.co.uk